Inspirati

BIG MOUTH POETRY

A little poetry with a LOT to say!

Gwendolyn Sharp Green

BIG MOUTH POETRY Inspirational Poems
A little poetry with a LOT to say!

Copyright © 2020 Gwendolyn Sharp Green
Published by Divine Favors Books Publications

All Rights Reserved. This book or parts thereof may not be reproduced, stored in a retrieval system, or transmitted in any form or by any means electronic, mechanical, photocopying, recording, or otherwise-without prior written permission from the author.

Dedication
This book is dedicated to my beloved husband, our amazing children, wonderful grandchildren, and future generations to come

TABLE OF CONTENTS	PAGE
Dedication	3
Don't Let the Devil Ride (Part I)	9
Don't Let the Devil Ride (Part II)	14
The Power of Prayer	20
My Cup is Filled with Tears, Until They Evaporate	23
Place Your Trust in Jesus	26
Simply Love	29
What is it, Do You Know?	33
Is Anything Too Hard for God	37
How Awesome is Our God!	40
A Word to the Wise	44
Merely Chatter	48
If Someone Would	51
Consistency	55
God Lifted Me	58
Let God Who Created You Go Before You	61
True Friendship	64
True Friendship Is	67
Sentimental Thoughts	70
The Early Morning Sky	73
I Know Love	77
Blind Eyes	80
Hey You, Get Your Head Out Of That Cloud	83
When I Get to Heaven	87
If I Could Sing!	90
Innocence	94
Mack – Life in America	97
Whose Child is This	101
SHE	106
	Cont.

TABLE OF CONTENTS	PAGE
The Watcher	109
Just Thank Him!	113
Grandma	117
Forever Memories	121
My Childhood Memories	125
Why Can't I Be Who I Want to Be???	130
The Finish Line	134
Great Words of Wisdom	139

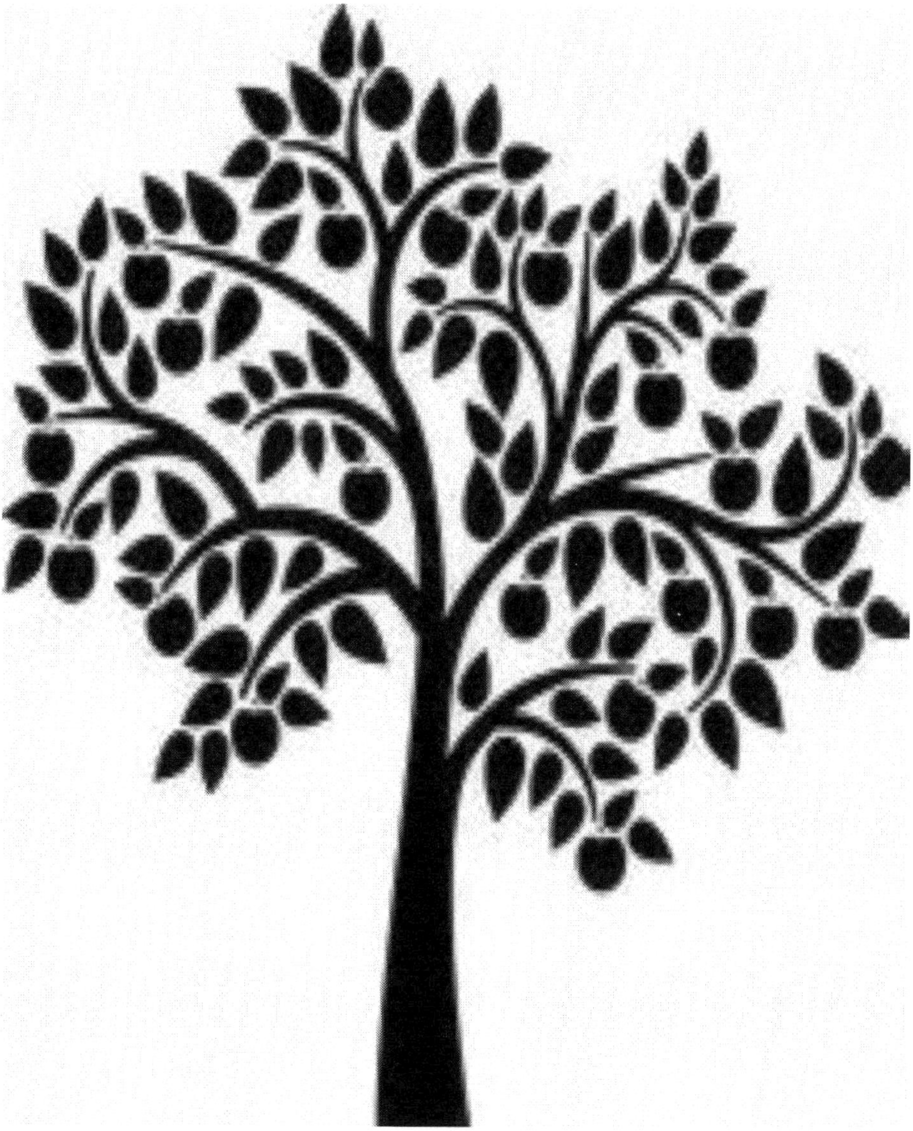

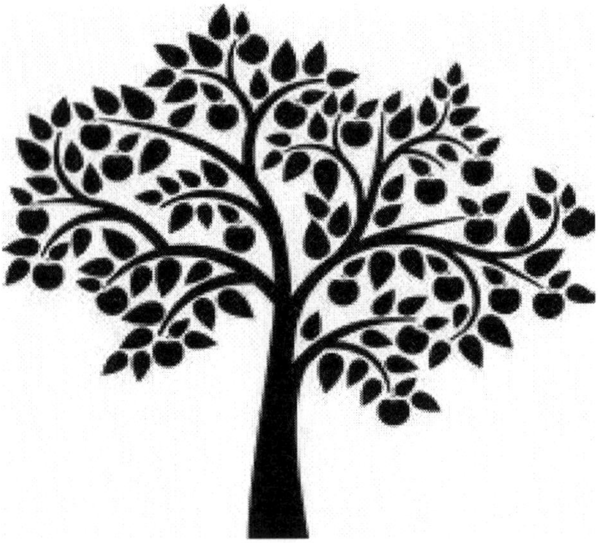

Be self-controlled and alert. Your enemy the devil prowls around like a roaring lion looking for someone to devour. 1 Peter 5:8 (NIV)

Don't Let the Devil Ride (Part I)

His ultimate goal is to steal, kill, and destroy
Never give-in to his devilish ploy
He's clever, slick, and quick
He's always up to a devilish trick

Keep your guard up always, as you should
The devil will never do anything good!

Just when nothing seems to be going your way
And you're feeling real down
He'll throw you a dreadful punch
And knock you to the ground
      And
Just when you're having the best day of your life
And everything is going just right
He'll catch you at your most vulnerable moment
Your best day will become your darkest night

He'll send you into a tailspin as fast as the speed of light
You won't be able to determine
Your left from your right

Don't let the devil ride!

He'll present you with challenges that are hard to face
He wants to make your entire life a shame and a disgrace

He'll deceive you into thinking that he's on your side
He'll take you on the most dangerous ride
Don't let him fool you
His game is to confuse and use you

He struts many different outfits and faces
He shows up in the most unexpected places
He's called by many names
But if you remain sober and vigilant
You will know him just the same
You hold the power to beat the devil, at his own game

Don't let the devil ride!

Your precious soul you must defend
He wants to steer you into a **dead-end**

He was not able to conquer Jesus, he's not a God send
Don't ever get it twisted, he's not trying to be your friend
He's only trying to capture and entrap you
To be destroyed with him in the end

He knows oh so well, that his destination is **hell**
And he wants to take you there, as well

There's not a soul in the world that he wants to spare
Don't give him the utmost pleasure, of driving you there

Don't let the devil ride!

His eyes are on many
He's not settling for just a few

However, this decision is all left up to you

Never ever allow that old evil devil the victory of defeat
For as long as you allow God to be your guide
You've got the devil beat

―――――――――――――――――――

Don't Let the Devil Ride (Part I)

"Self-Reflection"

What message did you get from the poem and the accompanying bible verse? How can you apply that message to your life?

_____
_____
_____
_____
_____
_____
_____
_____
_____
_____
_____
_____
_____
_____
_____
_____
_____
_____
_____
_____
_____
_____
_____
_____
_____

Again, the devil took him to a very high mountain and showed him all the Kingdoms of the world and their splendor. "All this I will give to you," he said, "If you will bow down and worship me." Jesus said to him, "Away from me, Satan!" For it is written: Worship the Lord your God, and serve him only." Then the Devil left him, and angels came and attended him.
Matthew 4:8 (NIV)

Don't Let the Devil Ride (Part II)

These are the things that the devil wants to entice you to do, as well as, what he desires to do to you. These are also the reasons that you must disavow him and never allow him to ride with you:

He wants to develop a bond with you
He has no limits as to what he will attempt to do
His mindset is such, that he has too many tricks
And his followers are too few

As fast as he can get your attention
He would like to fill your life
With an abundance of contention and dissension

Don't let the devil ride!

Don't forget, he's clever, slick, and double quick
He won't ever fail to use his repertoire
Of devilish tricks

He has as many old tricks as he has new
And he knows exactly which tricks
Are especially suitable to you
This is another reason why the devil
Would like nothing more, than to hitch a ride with you

Don't let the devil ride!

He strives on the weak in spirit
And those struggling in the flesh
He will delight in making your life, a living mess

He's quite capable of making the sweetest
Most pleasant aroma stink
His every move is well thought out
And planned to the very brink

His easiest prey and most sought out
Is unmistakably, the weakest link

SAINTS BEWARE! He knows your thoughts
Better than you will ever think
Never give that old sneaky devil a nod or a wink

Don't let the devil ride!

He does not discriminate
He'll take whomever he can make or break
Specifically, for his own devilish sake

He can display an attitude
As sweet as a sugar plum cake

His disguises are too numerous
His appearances are exclusively fake
Don't ever underestimate that old evil devil
He won't make any mistakes

Whenever he knows that you have found him out
He'll change his appearance and wait for you at the next route
Assuredly, without a doubt
Because this is what that old tricky devil is all about

Don't let the devil ride!

Access to the devil should always be denied
Be wise!
His actions and behavior you must learn to recognize
Have faith in Almighty God!
Ask him to be your guide
And let your faith in God, be well complied

Whatever you do and wherever you go
Don't let the devil ride!

Every time that the devil attempts to take a seat
Snatch the rug out from under his feet
He absolutely won't stop at anything
Until his devilment is complete
Until he takes the wheel
And you are in the passenger's seat

He will turn your very good visions
Into very bad decisions

He aims to destroy, and smear your good name
He would like nothing more than for you to be a shining star
In the devil's hall of shame

Yes, it is true
Life is filled with so many challenges
That we all will meet and face

The good news is

Through our Lord and Savior, Jesus Christ
God has granted us salvation and grace

In him (our Lord) always, we must trust and obey
Stay the course, and finish the race

Never forget, we all have a precious soul to defend

We are exclusively created by our **FATHER GOD**
We are all a God send

We have a Crown of Glory waiting for us, at the very end.
Amen!

_____

Don't Let the Devil Ride (Part II)

"Self-Reflection"

What message did you get from the poem and the accompanying bible verse? How can you apply that message to your life?

_____
_____
_____
_____
_____
_____
_____
_____
_____
_____
_____
_____
_____
_____
_____
_____
_____
_____
_____
_____
_____
_____
_____
_____
_____

Pray continually; give thanks in all circumstances, for this is God's will for you in Christ Jesus.   1Thessalonians 5:17-18 (NIV)

The Power of Prayer

Keep Praying

Pray for me and I'll pray for you
There is so much power in what prayer can do
Prayer can forever rescue you
Prayer can turn lives around and make them anew

There are no challenges in life that prayer cannot see you through, In times of stress, turmoil and danger
Never to prayer should you be a stranger

Prayer can give you guidance when there is no direction
Whenever you make a mistake in life
Prayer can make a correction
When you've lost contact with God
Prayer can make a connection

If ever in life you feel trapped, subdued, and in a worldly place
Prayer can give you restoration and amazing grace

There can never be too many prayers
But there can be too few
There is never a limit to what a prayer can do

───────────────

The Power of Prayer

"Self-Reflection"

What message did you get from the poem and the accompanying bible verse? How can you apply that message to your life?

_____
_____
_____
_____
_____
_____
_____
_____
_____
_____
_____
_____
_____
_____
_____
_____
_____
_____
_____
_____
_____
_____
_____
_____
_____
_____
_____
_____

My Cup is Filled with Tears, Until They Evaporate

For your name's sake, O Lord, preserve my life; in your righteousness, bring me out of trouble. Psalm 143: 11 (NIV)

Who can foresee what life will bring through the years?
We do know that life can bring joy, and life can bring tears
We do know that in life, we must face our strife and our fears

The trouble that life brings cannot be erased, only faced
Faced head-on, until trouble is gone
Sometimes gone for a reason, sometimes gone for a season

Although life will never be fully understood
Contribute to life the best that you could
Trouble will never be gone for good

Who knows why? Neither you nor I; only God!

Do not worry about life's woes that cannot be erased,
or put on hold
Do not worry about those matters in life that you cannot
untangle or fold
Do, focus on those matters in life, that you can control

Life is created on reality; life is not formed from pretense
Life is complicated, it is perplexing to comprehend
One certainty about life, is that life has an end

My Cup is Filled with Tears, Until They Evaporate

"Self-Reflection"

What message did you get from the poem and the accompanying bible verse? How can you apply that message to your life?

_____
_____
_____
_____
_____
_____
_____
_____
_____
_____
_____
_____
_____
_____
_____
_____
_____
_____
_____
_____
_____
_____
_____
_____
_____
_____
_____
_____
_____
_____
_____

**The Lord is my strength and my shield; my heart trusts in him and I am helped. My heart leaps for joy and I will give thanks to him in song.
Psalm 28:7 (NIV)**

Place Your Trust in Jesus

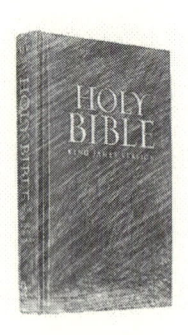

We have a friend in Jesus
He's with us everyday
He helps us through our struggles
As we journey day by day

In His word we must abide
He will forever be by our side
He stays with us through thick and thin
Keeping His promises until the end

And if we stay in Jesus
If we pray to him each day
If we let him order our steps
During our journey on our way

If we help others along the way
If we love our neighbors as we love ourselves
If we let our light shine everyday
He'll let nothing come our way, that will lead us astray

_____

Place Your Trust in Jesus

"Self-Reflection"

What message did you get from the poem and the accompanying bible verse? How can you apply that message to your life?

_____
_____
_____
_____
_____
_____
_____
_____
_____
_____
_____
_____
_____
_____
_____
_____
_____
_____
_____
_____
_____
_____
_____
_____
_____
_____
_____

We love because he first loved us. If anyone says, "I Love God," yet hates his brother, he is a liar. For anyone who does not love his brother, whom he has seen, cannot love God, whom he has not seen. And he has given us this command: Who ever loves God must also love his brother.
1 John 4:19-21 (NIV)

Simply Love

Love is kind
Love is sure
Love is clean
Love is pure
Love is yielding
Love is abiding
Love is giving
Love is striving

Love is hope
Love is faith
Love is unbought
Love is untaught
Love is spiritual
Love is real
Love is comforting
Love is healing
Love is unselfish
Love is willing

Love is as straight as a gate
Love is as gentle as a lamb
Love is as soft as a whisper
Yet, as loud as a trumpet
Love is God who watches over all from Heaven above

_____

Simply Love

"Self-Reflection"

What message did you get from the poem and the accompanying bible verse? How can you apply that message to your life?

_____
_____
_____
_____
_____
_____
_____
_____
_____
_____
_____
_____
_____
_____
_____
_____
_____
_____
_____
_____
_____
_____
_____
_____
_____
_____
_____
_____

And now these three remain: faith, hope and love. But the greatest of these Is love.   1Corinthians 13:13 (NIV)

What Is It, Do You Know?

It never dies
It's a tie that binds
It's a chain that never breaks
It's not fake
It's far from a mistake
It's more solid than steel
It's a door that never closes
It's as tall as the tallest mountain
It's like a beautiful steady running fountain

What is it, do you know?

It's like a roller coaster that won't let you off
When you start to feel as if it's letting you down
It picks you up, it will never let you touch the ground
It never leaves you, it stays around

Sometimes you try to loosen It, but it won't let you go
It's sealed as tight as the strongest glue
It's like your shadow, it stays with you

It's like a river that runs deep
It's beyond the sky
It's as genuine as a diamond
It's as pure as solid gold
It's way down deep in your soul

You can find it, but you cannot lose it

Have you known, do you know, **True Love**

_____

What is it, Do You Know?

"Self-Reflection"

What message did you get from the poem and the accompanying bible verse? How can you apply that message to your life?

_____
_____
_____
_____
_____
_____
_____
_____
_____
_____
_____
_____
_____
_____
_____
_____
_____
_____
_____
_____
_____
_____
_____
_____
_____

"Come to me, all you who are weary and burdened, and I will give you rest. Take my yoke upon you and learn from me, I am gentle and humble in heart, and you will find rest for your souls, for my yoke is easy and my burden is light."   Matthew 11:28-30 (NIV)

Is Anything Too Hard for God

The answer to the problem is not in the bottle
It's not in the throttle
It's not in the throttle combined with the bottle

Yes, this may sound confusing
However, never resort to using loosely
That which God has given to you, so profusely

No, this is not an illusion
There's a solution to the confusion

Yes, life comes with many woes and sorrows
And there are no guarantees of tomorrows

When life is tough, and your burdens are too hard
Surrender them to Father God

His arms are always opened, and waiting patiently for you
There is never anything too hard, for Father God to do

Is Anything too Hard for God

"Self-Reflection"

What message did you get from the poem and the accompanying bible verse? How can you apply that message to your life?

_____
_____
_____
_____
_____
_____
_____
_____
_____
_____
_____
_____
_____
_____
_____
_____
_____
_____
_____
_____
_____
_____
_____
_____
_____

How great you are, O Sovereign Lord! There is no one like you, and there is no God but you, as we have heard with our own ears.   2 Samuel 7:22 (NIV)

How Awesome is Our God!

He can make us rich
He can make us poor
He can give us less
He can give us more
He can open and shut any door

He gives us light, He gives us dark
He created the world where we all embark
He has given us a land of plenty
That is beyond the state-of-the-art
A world for our journey, a place to make our mark

There isn't anything that our father cannot do
What He does for me, He'll do for you

To love the Lord our God, to walk in his ways
To trust and obey him, all our lifelong days
Is all that he desires for us to do

To each of us He gives our own private line
A line which is always open in only his direction

He gives us love, mercy, grace, and protection
Above all, He has given to us his one and only begotten son
Our Lord and Savior Jesus Christ, who makes these connections

He once walked this earth as lowly man
And back to heaven He did ascend
He is Alpha and Omega, the beginning, and the end. Amen

_____

How Awesome is Our God!

"Self-Reflection"

What message did you get from the poem and the accompanying bible verse? How can you apply that message to your life?

_____
_____
_____
_____
_____
_____
_____
_____
_____
_____
_____
_____
_____
_____
_____
_____
_____
_____
_____
_____
_____
_____
_____
_____
_____
_____
_____

A wise man's heart guides his mouth, and his lips promote instruction. Pleasant words are a honeycomb, sweet to the soul and healing to the bones.   Proverbs 16:23-24 (NIV)

A Word to the Wise

treat people with Kindness

As you travel on life's most challenging journey...

Pay close attention to what you do and what you say
You never know who you'll meet along the way
Or, how and who's watching you from day to day

Watch how you meet and greet all people
As you pass their way

It's not always what you choose to do that matters
But It's sometimes what you choose to say

It's not always what you choose to say that matters
But it's sometimes what you choose to do

Always give respect to others
And they should give respect back to you

It does not matter who you are
But what matters is what you say and do

What matters the **most** is what you do and say to someone
And, what someone says and does to you
Be kind, respectful, learn to live and live to learn

Remember that whatever you get out of life
Depends on what to life you give

So, watch what you do, watch what you say
Give respect to all people along the way

And most importantly, pray for others each day
As you bless others, blessings will also come your way
_____

A Word to the Wise

"Self-Reflection"

What message did you get from the poem and the accompanying bible verse? How can you apply that message to your life?

_____
_____
_____
_____
_____
_____
_____
_____
_____
_____
_____
_____
_____
_____
_____
_____
_____
_____
_____
_____
_____
_____
_____
_____

So, we fix our eyes not on what is seen, but what is unseen. For what is seen is temporary, but what is unseen is eternal.
2 Corinthians 4:18 (NIV)

Merely Chatter

Is that you, are those yours
Is that your walk
Is that your talk
Are those your lips
Are those your hips
Is that your face
Is that your waist
Are those your nails, your ponytails
What is real anymore
What is appeal anymore
Who is fulfilled
What is true
What is mostly glue
If this is not you, do you know who
Is there a clue
Is anyone satisfied or perhaps gratified
This is merely chatter, does it matter?
_____
Merely Chatter

"Self-Reflection"

What message did you get from the poem and the accompanying bible verse? How can you apply that message to your life?

_____
_____
_____
_____
_____
_____
_____
_____
_____
_____
_____
_____
_____
_____
_____
_____
_____
_____
_____
_____
_____
_____
_____
_____
_____
_____

I can do everything through him who gives me strength.
  Philippians 4:13 (NIV)

IF SOMEONE WOULD

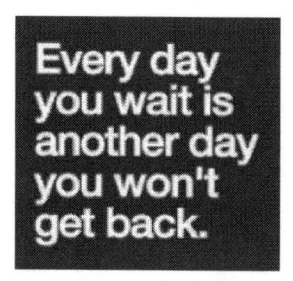

> Every day you wait is another day you won't get back.

Success is walking by; someone watches as it passes
Someone realized that it may never pass their way again
So that someone reached out and grabbed hold of it
Was that someone you?

Someone showed up when there were too few
That someone made a difference
Is that someone you?

Someone waits for their ship to come in but don't know when
Is that someone you?
Someone seeks its arrival and knows when
Is that someone you?

Someone showed up late and couldn't get in
Is that someone you?
Someone showed up on time and got through
Is that someone you?

Someone figured it all out
Is that someone you?
Someone didn't have a clue
Is that someone you?

Someone looked at what they were going through
Is that someone you?

Someone looked at what they were going to
Is that someone you?

Someone said, "I give up"
Is that someone you?
Someone said, "I'll try again"
Is that someone you?

Someone looked at the regrets of losing
Is that someone you?
Someone looked at the rewards of winning
Is that someone you?

Someone said, "I think I can"
Is that someone you?
Someone said, "I think I will"
Is that someone you?

If not now, when
If not you, who?

———————————
If Someone Would

"Self-Reflection"

What message did you get from the poem and the accompanying bible verse? How can you apply that message to your life?

_____
_____
_____
_____
_____
_____
_____
_____
_____
_____
_____
_____
_____
_____
_____
_____
_____
_____
_____
_____
_____
_____
_____
_____
_____
_____
_____
_____

Let us not become weary in doing good, for at the proper time we will reap a harvest if we do not give up. Galatians 6:9 (NIV)

Consistency

I arise faithfully each morning
Before the break of day
Soon I'm headed for the freeway

I'm always on my way
To earn another day's pay

Just the moonlit sky and I, I wonder why

Consistency

Oftentimes, I want to say, forget today's pay
But this is life's way, which is why I must be on my way
After all, it's just another day

What can I say?

I stare at the still moonlit sky, I wonder why

It's all about another day's pay
I must be on my way, no time to delay

As the earth rotates on its axis
Soon it will be another day

What can I say?

_____

Consistency

"Self-Reflection"

What message did you get from the poem and the accompanying bible verse? How can you apply that message to your life?

I will exalt you, O Lord, for you lifted me out of the depth and did not let my enemies gloat over me. O Lord my God, I called to you for help and you healed me. Psalm 30:1-2 (NIV)

God Lifted Me

On this bright and sunny day
Everyone is going about in their own determined way
Even though this is what I see, I can only speak for me

Here I sit in a horrible dream
A dream which has become a reality
A reality of loneliness, mental pain, and sorrow
A reality of gloom, doom, and horror

I cannot imagine a brighter tomorrow
Because I cannot see past today

I long for an awakening, except, I am not sleep
So, I humbly asked, "Lord why me, please set me free"

Then out of God's love and compassion

He lifted me
_____
God Lifted Me

"Self-Reflection"

What message did you get from the poem and the accompanying bible verse? How can you apply that message to your life?

_____
_____
_____
_____
_____
_____
_____
_____
_____
_____
_____
_____
_____
_____
_____
_____
_____
_____
_____
_____
_____
_____
_____
_____
_____
_____
_____

Trust in the Lord with all your heart and lean not on your own understanding; in all your ways acknowledge him, and he will make your paths straight.   Proverbs 3: 5-6 (NIV)

Let God Who Created You Go Before You

Let God be your guide
So that you can unmistakably decide

Consult with God first and foremost
In everything that you venture to do

Let God make that first big step
So that you can make the next two

Let God give you your very good vision
Before you make that very next decision

He'll give you something to grow on
So that you can continue to go on

Listen to God's voice, before you make that choice
Then, rejoice!
_____
Let God Who Created You Go Before You

"Self-Reflection"

What message did you get from the poem and the accompanying bible verse? How can you apply that message to your life?

_____
_____
_____
_____
_____
_____
_____
_____
_____
_____
_____
_____
_____
_____
_____
_____
_____
_____
_____
_____
_____
_____
_____
_____
_____

Two are better than one, because they have a good return for their work: If one falls down, his friend can help him up. But pity the man who falls and has no one to help him up! Ecclesiastes 4:9-10 (NIV)

True Friendship

True friendship originates from a very deep place

True friendship is a treasure that can never be replaced
It carries many fine qualities, such as sincerity, charm and grace

True friendship is as strong as a precious stone
It is the bond between friends, that sets the friendship tone

Once that bond has been set, regardless of how close or how far away
True friendship will never be broken, it will last forever and a day

To find true friendship is like finding a precious stone,
a diamond if you will, they both appreciate with timing,
they both are uniquely real

_____
True Friendship

"Self-Reflection"

What message did you get from the poem and the accompanying bible verse? How can you apply that message to your life?

_____
_____
_____
_____
_____
_____
_____
_____
_____
_____
_____
_____
_____
_____
_____
_____
_____
_____
_____
_____
_____
_____
_____
_____
_____
_____

True Friendship is:

Pure
Real
Exceptional
Cherishable
Irreplaceable
Oneness
Unique
Solid

Dazzling
Inspiring
Authentic
Most valuable
Outstanding
Nice
Delightful

_____

True Friendship Is

"Self-Reflection"

What message did you get from the poem and the accompanying bible verse? How can you apply that message to your life?

_____
_____
_____
_____
_____
_____
_____
_____
_____
_____
_____
_____
_____
_____
_____
_____
_____
_____
_____
_____
_____
_____
_____
_____
_____
_____
_____
_____

Then the Lord made a woman from the rib he had taken out of man, and he brought her to the man.   **Genesis 2:22 (NIV)**

Sentimental Thoughts

I am as much a part of you,
as you are a part of me.

I think of you each day,
I'd guess you think of me, in the same way.

I sometimes know your thoughts,
as you sometimes know mine.

Isn't it funny that two minds can be so inter-twined
as yours and mine.
_____

Sentimental Thoughts

"Self-Reflection"

What message did you get from the poem and the accompanying bible verse? How can you apply that message to your life?

_____
_____
_____
_____
_____
_____
_____
_____
_____
_____
_____
_____
_____
_____
_____
_____
_____
_____
_____
_____
_____
_____
_____
_____
_____
_____
_____
_____

For since the creation of the world God's invisible qualities-his eternal power and divine nature-have been clearly seen, being understood from what has been made, so that men are without excuse.   Romans 1:20 (NIV)

The Early Morning Sky

There is so much to see in the birth of a new sky
Exactly what is seen by individual minds and eyes
Depends solely upon how the imagination flies

Early to bed, early to rise
To count each mystery in the skies
One -by-one you count each mystique
As each one is quite unique
Some you will never see again
Not even in a millennium

Rise early my child and enjoy the wonders
Each is as mysterious as thunder

As your imagination starts to fly
It lets us know that God is near by

Come into my world and embark upon the beauty of nature
Travel with me into the universe
And stretch your imagination
Come enjoy the ride
Let your conscience be your guide

Sit back, relax, have a cup of tea
Or whatever uplifts your fantasy
Come enjoy this beautiful sky with me
You are visibly in great company

After all, these wonders are put there for us to see
God created this spectacular universe
From 'Sea to Shining Sea'

I am just a passer-by with my eyes on the sky
_____
The Early Morning Sky

"Self-Reflection"

What message did you get from the poem and the accompanying bible verse? How can you apply that message to your life?

_____
_____
_____
_____
_____
_____
_____
_____
_____
_____
_____
_____
_____
_____
_____
_____
_____
_____
_____
_____
_____
_____
_____
_____
_____
_____

Give thanks to the Lord, for he is good. His love endures forever.
Psalm 136:1 (NIV)

I Know Love

I know love
Deep, dying, passionate love
I know love
Enchanting, romantic, ecstatic love
I know love
Modern, new, unfashionable love
I know love
Demanding, possessive, aggressive love
I know love
Unfinished, diminished, replenished love
I know love
Denied, implied, inspired love
I know love
Rehearsed, coerced, reversed love
I know love
Misguided, slighted, divided love
I know love
Forgiven, driven, forbidden love
I know love
Amazing, enraging, star gazing love
I know love
Heightened, brightened, enlightened love
I know love
Hypnotizing, mesmerizing, uncompromising love
I know love
Yet, there is none as genuine as EVERLASTING love
I know love

_____

I Know Love

"Self-Reflection"

What message did you get from the poem and the accompanying bible verse? How can you apply that message to your life?

_____
_____
_____
_____
_____
_____
_____
_____
_____
_____
_____
_____
_____
_____
_____
_____
_____
_____
_____
_____
_____
_____
_____
_____
_____
_____

Let us acknowledge the Lord; let us press on to acknowledge him. As surely as the sun rises he will appear; he will come to us like the winter rains, like the spring rains that water the earth. Hosea 6:3 (NIV)

Blind Eyes

Once I was blind but now, I clearly see,
the wonderful blessings that you poured on me.
Once I was lost in sorrow and shame,
I sought you and found you, now my life has forever changed.
          And
One day as I knelt and started to pray,
Love touched me in a wonderful way.
Suddenly, I felt a burden had been lifted
And into your arms I found that I had shifted.

I felt a warmth of peace flow into my soul.
I knew that I was being made whole.
All my pressure and strain had gone,
I knew in my heart that a victory had been won.

I had been advanced to a new level.
          And
Now at last my arms I can raise
In love, worship, thanksgiving, and praise.
All that I owe I could never repay,
You entered my life and showed me the way.

Blind Eyes

"Self-Reflection"

What message did you get from the poem and the accompanying bible verse? How can you apply that message to your life?

_____
_____
_____
_____
_____
_____
_____
_____
_____
_____
_____
_____
_____
_____
_____
_____
_____
_____
_____
_____
_____
_____
_____
_____
_____
_____
_____
_____
_____
_____

Then Peter began to speak: "I now realize how true it is that God does not show favoritism but accepts men from every nation who fear him and do what is right." Acts 10:34 (NIV)

Hey You, Get Your Head Out Of That Cloud

You have got some coming and some going
Some wondering and some knowing
Some appear to accept the words you have said
Others are scratching their heads
You choose this one over that one, that one over this one.

Listen, you one, who do you think you are?
You are by far from who you think you are.

Take a good look in the mirror
Then you will see that person staring back at you, much clearer.

Your mind is playing tricks on you
Those coming and going
Wondering and knowing
And others, are very much like you

You are nothing more than them
And they are nothing more than you
You are all created by one and the same
Father God Almighty is his name.

Love who you are so that you can love who they are.

Be true to yourself.
_____
Hey You, Get Your Head Out Of That Cloud

"Self-Reflection"

What message did you get from the poem and the accompanying bible verse? How can you apply that message to your life?

_____
_____
_____
_____
_____
_____
_____
_____
_____
_____
_____
_____
_____
_____
_____
_____
_____
_____
_____
_____
_____
_____
_____
_____
_____
_____
_____
_____

He will wipe every tear from their eyes. There will be no more death or mourning or crying or pain, for the old order of things has passed away.
Revelation 21:4 (NIV)

When I Get to Heaven

When I get to heaven this is what I am going to say:

Hello God, how do you do
Lord, I am so overjoyed to be with you

I've waited my whole life long
To see you sitting on your beautiful throne
To tell you how happy I am to make Heaven my eternal home

Please Lord, take my hand, as humbly before you I stand
Never another tear or sorrow, never another tomorrow

No more pain, no frets, no regrets
No disappointments or tears, no pouting, no doubting
Just worship, praise, and glorious shouting

At last, at last, my soul has been set free
I've reached my final destination-eternity
Where every day will always be the same
Thanks be to you Father God; I will forever praise your holy name. Amen

_____

When I Get to Heaven

"Self-Reflection"

What message did you get from the poem and the accompanying bible verse? How can you apply that message to your life?

_____
_____
_____
_____
_____
_____
_____
_____
_____
_____
_____
_____
_____
_____
_____
_____
_____
_____
_____
_____
_____
_____
_____
_____
_____
_____
_____

"Do not let your hearts be troubled. Trust in God, trust also in me. In my father's house are many rooms; if it were not so, I would have told you. I am going there to prepare a place for you. And if I go and prepare a place for you, I will come back and take you to be with me that you also may be where I am. You know the place where I am going."   John 14:1-4 (NIV)

If I Could Sing!

If I could sing!

I'd sing away the blues from lonely souls
I'd sing in the good news of what is new and old
Oh, how I wish that I could sing!

If I could sing!

I'd sing out all hatred from every hate filled heart
And I'd sing in universal love, right from the start
My voice would be heard near and far
And all over the world

If I could sing!

I'd sing the sad out of every today and tomorrow
No one will ever linger with any sorrow

If I could sing!

I'd sing in the sunshine on cloudy days
And I'd sing in the rain when the land is thirsty
There would be "Songbirds" perched in every tree
And they would harmonize so beautifully with me

If only I could sing!

'Let freedom ring, let freedom ring,' all over the world
Let freedom be heard in the ears of every man, woman, boy and girl

Oh, how I wish that I could sing!

_____

If I Could Sing!

"Self-Reflection"

What message did you get from the poem and the accompanying bible verse? How can you apply that message to your life?

_____
_____
_____
_____
_____
_____
_____
_____
_____
_____
_____
_____
_____
_____
_____
_____
_____
_____
_____
_____
_____
_____
_____
_____
_____

You made all the delicate, inner parts of my body and knit me together in my mother's womb.   Psalm 139:13 (NIV)

Innocence

The nearest soul on earth to an Angel we will ever see,
is that of a newborn BABY
such joy to have, so precious to behold.

Thank you, dear God, for sending this little soul.

So perfectly formed by God's own hand,
exactly how this is done is a mystery to man.

A manner as free as a bird flying gracefully in the air,
not a single worry, not a single care.

Eyes as beautiful and bright as the morning star,
that gazes upon you with the most innocent stare,
an innocence from the beginning that is purely rare.

Innocence

No hatred, no prejudice, or malice filled heart,
only pure love, joy, and sincerity from the start.

Both a father and a mother's pride,
may God forever be by their side, and
may in God's word will they always abide.

Innocence

"Self-Reflection"

What message did you get from the poem and the accompanying bible verse? How can you apply that message to your life?

_____
_____
_____
_____
_____
_____
_____
_____
_____
_____
_____
_____
_____
_____
_____
_____
_____
_____
_____
_____
_____
_____
_____
_____
_____
_____
_____
_____
_____

He gives strength to the weary and increases the power of the weak. Even youths grow tired and weary, and young men stumble and fall; but those who hope in the Lord will renew their strength. They will soar on wings like eagles; they will run and not grow weary, they will walk and not be faint.
Isaiah 40:29-31 (NIV)

Mack – Life in America

I see you walking with your backpack, knapsack
And looking kind of whack like
As if you don't know what to do
You don't have the slightest clue
You're looking all confused and used
Walking to and fro, don't know which way to go
Life has dealt you a terrible blow

Each day is more defeating and you're constantly repeating,
"If someone would please, just open up a door,
this life, I abhor, I can't take this anymore."

You're wishing that you had stayed in school
Echoing that you must have been a fool
For thinking that school wasn't cool
Wishing that you had followed the rules
Now you need a new pair of shoes

You're feeling extremely frustrated
Wondering why you're so aggravated
If only you had waited
Life seems so ill fated

You're so hungry, you need to be fed
You're so tired, you need a bed
You're remembering when your mother said,

"You can be anything that you want to be,
do anything that you want to do; it is all left up
to you."

You never felt so degraded, so underrated
Wishing that you had concentrated
More on how you could have made it
Boy, don't you hate it!

Now you're feeling so betrayed,
wishing that you had stayed and played.
Allowed yourself to become a man
A man who can stand, on his own two feet,
So, you begin regretfully to repeat
"What the heck, I can't compete,
I'm sick and tired of defeat,
disappointment is all that I meet."

Son, your life is not complete
You have a challenge that you need to meet

Don't be caught an old man,
With your head buried in the sand
You must first take a stand
Need to get yourself a plan
You just need a helping hand

You can turn your life around, be the proudest man in town
Get yourself up off that ground!
Never let anything turn you up-side-down
So much of your life has yet to be found

Don't be the author of hate, it's not too late
You can still determine your fate
This is what makes living in America so great!

Mack – Life in America

"Self-Reflection"

What message did you get from the poem and the accompanying bible verse? How can you apply that message to your life?

_____
_____
_____
_____
_____
_____
_____
_____
_____
_____
_____
_____
_____
_____
_____
_____
_____
_____
_____
_____
_____
_____
_____
_____
_____

Children, obey your parents in the Lord, for this is right. "Honor your father and mother" which is the first commandment with a Promise-that it may go well with you, and you may enjoy long life on the earth." Father's do not exasperate your children; instead bring them up in the training and instruction of the Lord.   Ephesians 6:1-3 (NIV)

Whose Child is This

Today, I saw a young man being handcuffed by two Law Enforcement Officers, it touched my heart.
I asked myself the following: (true story)

Why-why has a child gone astray
Where-where are his people
Who- who would want their child to be treated in such a way
When-when in this child's life did a situation go wrong
What- what can be done to prevent these kind of situations
(difficult questions to answer, I know)

Is this happening to some of our children because
Maybe they have not been taught right from wrong
Or has discipline been absent from the home too long
Something has gone terribly wrong

A household should be two-parents strong, when possible
Neither parent should be missing from a child's life too long
Children should be constantly taught right from wrong
Discipline without harm should be taught all year long

Parents, monitor your children each day
Devise a plan and teach them the rightful way
Do everything within your power to keep them from going astray

After all, it is a parent's duty to nourish and guide them along
Until they become physically, mentally, and emotionally strong

Take them to church on Sunday; Sunday school is cool
Whatever happened to teaching 'The Golden Rule'
Just ask God to guide you each and everyday
Do not let that precious life that you brought into this world
Be thrown away

Children come into this world without a clue
How are they to know when, where, why
And what to do
You see, a lot of who your child is or can become
Is sometimes left up to you
It's not so much about what a child does
It's what, for the child, that the parents can do

You don't need fortune or fame, it can be
as simple as giving your child a name; life is not a game

In essence, choosing to teach your child right from wrong
Disciplining without harm all year long
Choosing to have a two-parent home is free
These are God given rights for you and me
They should be passed from generation to generation
contagiously

Remember none of us are perfect
We are here to do God's will
We have been blessed with children
This was meant to be a thrill
Still, we owe to our children, the very best that we can give

Let us pray that they all live lives that are fulfilled
With everything in life for them
That is in God the Creator's will

A child should never be allowed to go astray
God did not intend for life to be that way
God knows that rearing a child is not easy to do
Seek help from him as He wants you to

He promises, always, to be with you
Have faith in Father God
He will surely see you through

This child could be mine; this child could be yours
This child needs to be loved and adored
_____
Whose Child is This

"Self-Reflection"

What message did you get from the poem and the accompanying bible verse? How can you apply that message to your life?

_____
_____
_____
_____
_____
_____
_____
_____
_____
_____
_____
_____
_____
_____
_____
_____
_____
_____
_____
_____
_____
_____
_____
_____
_____
_____

**Rich and poor have this in common: The Lord is the maker of them all.
Proverbs 22:2 (NIV)**

SHE

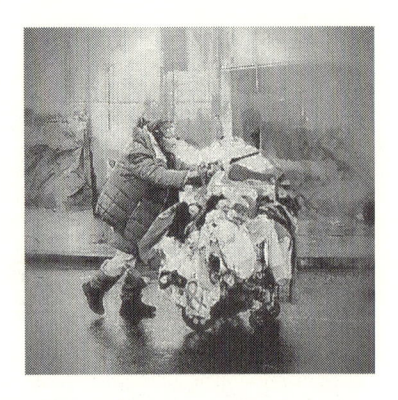

She has lost her beautiful smile.
She sleeps on a bench drenched in a stench.
She walks with a limp and a slight drag.
She carries all that she owns in a black bag.
Her beautiful hair is wrapped tight in a do-rag.
She seems to never have anything to say.

She rarely looks anyone in the eye.
Could it be that she's just shy?
Only she and God knows why.

People all around her come and go all day, every day;
And even though they see her, they look the other way.
Many of them know that she lives under the bridge,
In the park, and on the streets.

I often ponder...does anyone ever wonder, who is "She."
She could have been you; she could have been me.

SHE

"Self-Reflection"

What message did you get from the poem and the accompanying bible verse? How can you apply that message to your life?

_____
_____
_____
_____
_____
_____
_____
_____
_____
_____
_____
_____
_____
_____
_____
_____
_____
_____
_____
_____
_____
_____
_____
_____
_____
_____
_____
_____
_____
_____
_____

Do not forget to show hospitality to strangers, for by so doing some people have shown hospitality to angels without knowing it. Continue to remember those in prison as if you were together with them in prison, and those who are mistreated as if you yourselves were suffering.
Hebrews 13:2-3 (NIV)

The Watcher

Can you guess who I am?

I live my life one day at a time
I have a mother, I have a father

My heart beats the same rhythm as yours
My blood runs warm and freely through my veins
I am very much like you
Yet, I am different

I may be a mother, I may be a father
I am watched, I am a watcher
I see many coming and going from all walks of life

My dreams have been shattered and hope is dim
I greet the rising sun each day and bid farewell to the sunset
Day and night have no real meaning to me, you see

My life can be compared to that of a bird
Though the birds gaze down on me
I bathe in the sun and sometimes I am washed by the rain
Nature has become my best friend

But still, I find the courage to reach out to those who are like me
Because I am human, and some in turn reach out to me
I am still human, my fate and destiny are out of my control

Hunger is a way of life for me

I am always down
I spend a lot of time on the bare ground

I am weary and I am worn
I am admired by no one

I am known by many
But only a few know my real name
To many, I am better known as "The Homeless"
_____

The Watcher

"Self-Reflection"

What message did you get from the poem and the accompanying bible verse? How can you apply that message to your life?

_____
_____
_____
_____
_____
_____
_____
_____
_____
_____
_____
_____
_____
_____
_____
_____
_____
_____
_____
_____
_____
_____
_____
_____
_____
_____

Give thanks to the Lord, for he is good; his love endures forever.
1 Chronicles 16:34 (NIV)

Just Thank Him!

You can't come talking to God just any old kind of way
Humbly say what you mean and humbly mean what you say

Do not thank him some of the time
But thank him all day

Whether you are up, down, or hanging around
On the ocean, sea, or solid ground

    Just thank him

Whether you have self- confidence or self- doubt
Feeling speechless or wanting to shout

    Just thank him

Whether you are coming or going
Lacking knowledge or all knowing

    Just thank him

Whether you are walking, running, sitting or standing
Whether you are cruising, flying, or bracing for a landing

    Just thank him

Whether you are happy or sad
Or just plain glad

    Just thank him

He's front back and center
Come summer, spring, fall or winter

    Just thank him

He never waver, he's consistent,
Able and available

    Just thank him

He's on every shift
You ought to thank him for your gifts

    Just thank him

He showers us with love, blessings, and righteousness
Whether you feel you have more or less
Out of whatever you have, give to God your very best

    Just thank him

He's the author of truth and every good story
Give God the honor, praise, and the glory

    _____
    Just Thank Him!

"Self-Reflection"

What message did you get from the poem and the accompanying bible verse? How can you apply that message to your life?

_____
_____
_____
_____
_____
_____
_____
_____
_____
_____
_____
_____
_____
_____
_____
_____
_____
_____
_____
_____
_____
_____
_____
_____
_____
_____
_____
_____

Who is wise and understanding among you? Let him show it by his good life, by the deeds done in the humility that comes from wisdom.
James 4:15 (NIV)

Grandma

Some of the most cherished memories from
my past thus far, are during the wonderful years
that I shared with my grandma.

She always displayed a spirit that was kind, good and sweet
in my opinion, one that could not be beat, so to speak.
She was one of the nicest people that you would ever want to meet.

She was always willing to lend a helping hand
to any woman, child or man.
She often visited the sick and gave to the poor.
Her house was always an open door.

She always had something nice to say
to anyone who came her way.

She never wavered in her ways
not morning, noon, or night.
It seemed that she consistently
did everything just right.

Grandma could never do anything wrong
in my eyesight.

I can still envision her in my mind
as she always got on her knees to pray.
I can distinctly remember hearing her say,
"If it is the Lord's will, I shall live to see another day." Amen

_____
Grandma

"Self-Reflection"

What message did you get from the poem and the accompanying bible verse? How can you apply that message to your life?

_____
_____
_____
_____
_____
_____
_____
_____
_____
_____
_____
_____
_____
_____
_____
_____
_____
_____
_____
_____
_____
_____
_____
_____
_____
_____
_____

Train a child in the way he should go, and when he is old, he will not turn from it.   Proverbs 22:6 (NIV)

Forever Memories

I think about how

Things used to be
and how they are now,
how you used to call my name
and how I used to reply
how you used to look at me
and how I used to smile.

I think about how

We used to sit and talk
and while the time away,
and how at bedtime I bowed my head,
and how you taught me to pray.

'Now I lay me down to sleep,
I pray to the Lord my soul to keep.
If I should die before I awake,
I pray to the Lord my soul to take.' Amen

Although, the way things used to be
was quite some time ago
the memories of you still linger with me,
and will forever more.
          And
Regardless of how things used to be,
the cherishable impressions that you made on me
will never, ever cease to be.
          And
The love that I carry in my heart for you
will forever remain in me
all because of the undying love
that you have shown and given to me.

_____

Forever Memories

This poem was written in loving memory of my dear mother.

"Self-Reflection"

What message did you get from the poem and the accompanying bible verse? How can you apply that message to your life?

_____
_____
_____
_____
_____
_____
_____
_____
_____
_____
_____
_____
_____
_____
_____
_____
_____
_____
_____
_____
_____
_____
_____
_____
_____
_____

My Childhood Memories
A Saturday Evening Kind of Day
These are true memories based on my childhood
recollections of some of the most "Happy Days" of my life.

The sound of laughter can be heard near and far away.
Outside, children are bursting with energy as they play.
Mom and grandma sitting out on the porch
as a neighbor walking by stops to chat along the way.

Birds perched on a branch in the big oak tree, while
Mr. Owl sits deep in a hollow watching mysteriously.

Mr. Lee, (who was blind, guided by his stick in hand) said, "Hello Ladies," very hospitably; grandma nods her head forward, and replies, "Fine, thank you Mr. Lee," as he continues walking down the street, very poised and swiftly.

The children continued to run, jump, and play
while observing every passer-by who passed their way, hearing every spoken word, including what mom and grandma had to say.

Every now and then they'll cease to play
Just to hear what grandma had to say, because
"Grandma" speaks the most memorable and sweetest sounds
 of the day.

A picture of lemonade sits in the fridge as fresh baked
cookies cool on the table; we continue to rip, run, and jump,
making sounds of horses being let out of a stable.

You are waiting anxiously as you continue to play
to hear mom's voice eventually say, "Lemonade and cookies
are on the way, do you children ever get tired of running
back and forth every single day?" (only silence, no replies)

Occasionally, you would notice the beautiful flowers in
"Grandma's" flower garden, even stop to pluck a petal or two,
or whatever your young mind tells you to do,
wrap around a maple tree, stare at a honeybee,
play and sing the nursery rhyme, 'Ring around the roses,
a pocket full of posies.'

Dancing in fresh air, arms spread out like the wings of an eagle,
displaying the attitudes as that of an eager beaver.

Not a care in the world, feeling full of pure joy,
never a feeling of sorrow, no thoughts of tomorrow.

Soon the sun will begin to drift slowly away,
seeming to take with it all the sounds of the day.

No longer can you hear the laughter of children at play.
The streets are quieter, mom and grandma's rocking chairs no longer
sway.

The end is drawing near for yet another beautiful and precious day.

Night is approaching fast, and dark has arrived at last.

The only sounds that can be heard now is that of a dog's bark and far, far away, I hear sounds like those of a lark.
And every once in a while, I can hear grandpa make a remark.

It is now that I look forward to tomorrow.

Another wonderful day has ended, tomorrow will be just as splendid.

_____
My Childhood Memories
A Saturday Evening Kind of Day

"Self-Reflection"

What message did you get from the poem and the accompanying bible verse? How can you apply that message to your life?

_____
_____
_____
_____
_____
_____
_____
_____
_____
_____
_____
_____
_____
_____
_____
_____
_____
_____
_____
_____
_____
_____
_____
_____
_____
_____

For the entire law is fulfilled in keeping this one command: "Love your neighbor as yourself." Galatians 5:14 (NIV)

Why Can't I Be Who I Want to Be???

Why can't I walk down the streets in peace in the land of the free
Why can't I be who I want to be, rightfully exploring my liberty
Why am I being watched by judgmental eyes,
Being thought of as a vagrant or a thief

Why can't I express an emotion without having it declared as an
Angry explosion or a senseless noise
When it's just another expressive voice
 Is "Freedom of Speech" not my choice

On every road that I travel, there are stumbling blocks
I have knocked on too many doors
Only to discover that they are locked

Why is my life a continuous struggle and fight
Whatever happened to my "Unalienable Rights"

Why day in and day out am I faced with some form of frustration
Will I ever get justification

Why am I most likely the chosen one to have to step aside
Too often being stripped of my pride, and my human rights denied
Because by the rules some refuse to abide
Why do you think that God is not on my side

God made every man, woman and child, didn't he
Why am I too often treated unfairly and unequally
Why can't I respectfully be who I want to be

Too many whys, too many wrongs
These whys have gone unanswered much too long
The season is here to right these wrongs; why let it pass us by?

_____
Why Can't I Be Who I Want to Be???

"Hate is too heavy a burden, so we need to lay it down, it is better to love."   John Robert Lewis 1940-2020

This poem is dedicated to the late Congressman, John R. Lewis, who was an avid Freedom Fighter until the end of his life. May he rest in peace.

"Self-Reflection"

What message did you get from the poem and the accompanying bible verse? How can you apply that message to your life?

Therefore, since we are surrounded by such a great cloud of witnesses, let us throw off everything that hinders and the sin that so easily entangles, and let us run with perseverance the race marked out for us. Let us fix our eyes on Jesus, the author and perfecter of our faith, who for the joy set before him endured the cross, scorning its shame, and sat down at the right hand of the throne of God.   Hebrews 12:1-2 (NIV)

The Finish Line

Run, run, have no fear
Life is filled with lots of good cheer

As you listen to the rhythm of competitive feet
Keep in mind that you have a deadline to meet

This is all about you, yourself, and your stride
Don't worry about who is on the other side

Every trace in your face shows that you want to win
Let your personal wind take you for a spin

You can go places that you've never been

Remember what, who, how, and when
Keep on running, keep on running
Until the very end

Run, run, you look so sweet
You have an important deadline to beat
Keep your head up, body straight, follow your feet
Run, run, as if a pot of gold awaits you down the street
Run, run, until your race is complete

Run, run, give up, don't you dare
To thy own self, be fair
You've not a second to spare
Keep running, keep running
You are almost there

Run, run, you look so fine
As your feet crossed over the finished line

In this race, you have stayed the course
Your very name, God will endorse

You have made a legacy that will forever be defended
You have run this race until it ended
_____

The Finish Line

"Self-Reflection"

What message did you get from the poem and the accompanying bible verse? How can you apply that message to your life?

_____
_____
_____
_____
_____
_____
_____
_____
_____
_____
_____
_____
_____
_____
_____
_____
_____
_____
_____
_____
_____
_____
_____
_____
_____
_____
_____
_____

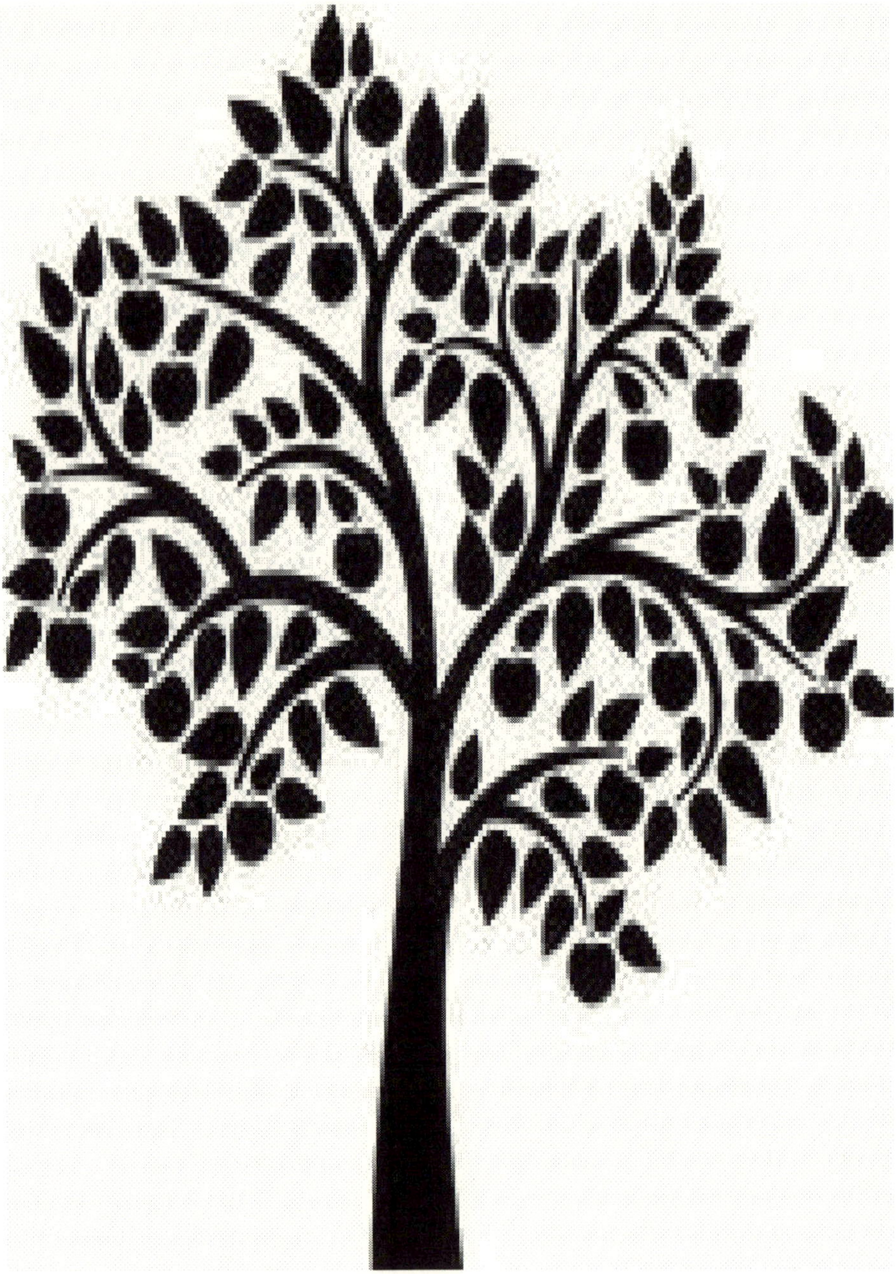

Great Words of Wisdom

To

Know

And

Grow

On

All scriptures are taken from the 'New International Version' (NIV) of the Holy Bible

Faithfulness

Deuteronomy 7:9
Know therefore that the Lord your God is God; he is the faithful God. Keeping his covenant of love to a thousand generations of those who love and keep his commandments.

2 Thessalonians 3:3
But the Lord is faithful, and he will strengthen you and protect you from the evil one.

Isaiah 25: 1
Lord, you are my God; I will exalt you and praise your name, for in perfect faithfulness you have done wonderful things, things planned long ago.

Psalm 91:4
He will cover you with his feathers, and under his wings you will find refuge; his faithfulness will be your shield and rampart.

1 John 1:9
If we confess our sins, he is faithful and just and will forgive us our sins and purify us from all unrighteousness.

Lamentations 3:22-23
Because of the Lord's great love, we are not consumed, for his compassions never fail. They are new every morning, great is your faithfulness.

Matthew 25:21
His master replied, 'Well done, good and faithful servant! You have been faithful with a few things; I will put you in charge of many things. Come and share your master's happiness!'

Forgiveness

Matthew 6:14-15
For if you forgive other people when they sin against you, your heavenly Father will also forgive you. But if you do not forgive others their sins, your Father will not forgive you.

Mark 11:25
And when you stand praying, if you hold anything against anyone, forgive them, so that your Father in heaven may forgive you your sins.

Colossians 3:13
Bear with each other and forgive whatever grievances you may have against one another. Forgive as the Lord forgave you.

Luke 6:37
"Do not judge, and you will not be judged. Do not condemn, and you will not be condemned. Forgive, and you will be forgiven."

Friends

Proverbs 27:9
Perfume and incense bring joy to the heart, and the pleasantness of one's friend springs from his earnest counsel.

Job 16:20-21
My intercessor is my friend as my eyes pour out tears to God; on behalf of man he pleads with God as one pleads for a friend.

Psalm 133-1
How good and pleasant it is when brothers live together in unity!

Ecclesiastes 4:9-10
Two are better than one, because they have a good return for their work: If one falls down, his friend can help him up. But pity the man who falls and has no one to help him up!

Proverbs 27:5-6
Better is open rebuke than hidden love. Wounds from a friend can be trusted, but an enemy multiplies kisses.

1Peter 3:8-9
Finally, all of you, be like-minded, be sympathetic, love one another, be compassionate and humble. Do not repay evil with evil or insult with insult. On the contrary, repay evil with blessing, because to this you were called so that you may inherit a blessing.

Justice

Zechariah 7:8-10
This is what the Lord Almighty said: 'Administer true justice; show mercy and compassion to one another. Do not oppress the widow or the fatherless, the foreigner or the poor. Do not plot evil against each other.'

Psalm 106:3
Blessed are they who maintain justice, who constantly do what Is right.

Micah 6:8
He has shown you, O mortal, what is good. And what does the Lord require of you? To act justly and to love mercy and to walk humbly with your God.

Deuteronomy 32:4
He is the rock, his works are perfect, and all his ways are just. A faithful God who does no wrong, upright and just is he.

Amos 5:24
But let justice roll on like a river, righteousness like a never-failing stream!

Love

Matthew 22:37-39
Jesus replied, "Love the Lord your God with all your heart and with all your soul and with all your mind. This is the first and greatest commandment. And the second is like it: Love your neighbor as yourself."

1 Peter 4:8
Above all, love each other deeply, because love covers over a multitude of sins.

Psalm 103:17-18
But from everlasting to everlasting the Lord's love is with those who fear him, and his righteousness with their children's children-with those who keep his covenant and remember to obey his precepts.

1 Corinthians 13:4-6
Love is patient, love is kind. It does not envy, it does not boast, it is not proud. It does not dishonor others, it is not self-seeking, it is not easily angered, it keeps no record of wrongs. Love does not delight in evil but rejoices with the truth.

Romans 12:9-10
Love must be sincere. Hate what is evil; cling to what is good. Be devoted to one another in brotherly love. Honor one another above yourselves.

1 Corinthians 16:13-14
Be on your guard; stand firm in the faith; be men of good courage; be strong. Do everything in love.

Wisdom

Proverbs 9:10-12
The fear of the Lord is the beginning of wisdom, and knowledge of the Holy one is understanding. For through wisdom your days will be many, and years will be added to your life. If you are wise, your wisdom will reward you; if you are a mocker, you alone will suffer.

Proverbs 4:5-6
Get wisdom, get understanding; do not forget my words or turn away from them. Do not forsake wisdom, and she will protect you; love her, and she will watch over you.

James 1:5-6
If any of you lacks wisdom, you should ask God, who gives generously to all without finding fault, and it will be given to you. But when you ask, you must believe and not doubt, because the one who doubts is like a wave of the sea, blown and tossed by the wind.

Proverbs 16-16
How much better to get wisdom than gold, to choose understanding rather than silver.

Colossians 4:5-6
Be wise in the way you act toward outsiders; make the most of every opportunity. Let your conversation be always full of grace, seasoned with salt, so that you may know how to answer everyone.

1 Corinthians 1:30
It is because of him that you are in Christ Jesus, who has become for us wisdom from God-that is, our righteousness, holiness and redemption.

Matthew 5:1-12

Now when Jesus saw the crowds, he went up on the Mountainside and sat down. His disciples came to him, and he began to teach them.

The Beatitudes

He said:

"Blessed are the poor in spirit, for theirs is the Kingdom of Heaven.

Blessed are those who mourn, for they shall be comforted.

Blessed are the meek, for they will inherit the earth.

Blessed are those who hunger and thirst for righteousness,

for they shall be filled.

Blessed are the merciful, for they shall be shown mercy.

Blessed are the pure in heart, for they shall see God.

Blessed are the peacemakers, for they shall be called children of God.

Blessed are those who are persecuted because of righteousness,

for theirs is the Kingdom of Heaven.

Blessed are you when people insult you, persecute you and falsely

say all kinds of evil against you because of me.

Rejoice and be glad, because great is your reward in Heaven,

for in the same way, they persecuted the prophets who were before you."

Psalm 23

A Psalm of David.

The Lord is my Shepherd, I lack for nothing.

He makes me lie down in green pastures,

he leads me beside quiet waters, he refreshes my soul.

Even though I walk through the darkest valley, I will fear

no evil, for you are with me; your rod and your staff,

they comfort me. You prepare a table before me in the

presence of my enemies. You anoint my head with oil,

my cup overflows. Surely your goodness and love will

follow me, all the days of my life, and I will dwell in the

house of the Lord forever.

Psalm 100

A psalm for giving thanks

Shout for joy to the Lord, all the earth. Worship the Lord with gladness; come before him with joyful songs. Know that the Lord is God. It is he who made us, and we are his; we are his people, the sheep of his pasture. Enter his gates with thanksgiving and his courts with praise; give thanks to him and praise his name. For the Lord is good and his love endures forever; his faithfulness continues through all generations.

Psalm 121

A song of ascents

I lift up my eyes to the hills-where does my help come from?

My help comes from the Lord, the Maker of heaven and earth.

He will not let your foot slip-he who watches over you will not slumber;

indeed, he who watches over Israel will neither slumber nor sleep.

The Lord watches over you-the Lord is your shade at your right hand;

the sun will not harm you by day, nor the moon by night.

The Lord will keep you from all harm-he will watch over your life;

the Lord will watch over your coming and going both now and forevermore.

The Golden Rule

"Do to others as you would have them do to you"

Luke 6:31

A Time for Everything

There is a time for everything, and a season for every activity under the heaven:

A time to be born and a time to die.
A time to plant and a time to uproot.
A time to kill and a time to heal.
A time to tear down and a time to build.
A time to weep and a time to laugh.
A time to mourn and a time to dance.
A time to scatter stones and a time to gather them.
A time to embrace and a time to refrain.
A time to search and a time to give up.
A time to keep and a time to throw away.
A time to tear and a time to mend.
A time to be silent and a time to speak.
A time to love and a time to hate.
A time for war and a time for peace.
What does the worker gain for his toil?
I have seen the burden God has laid on men.
He has made everything beautiful in its time.
He has also set eternity in the hearts of men; yet they
cannot fathom what God has done from beginning to end.
I know that there is nothing better for men than to be happy and
and do good while they live.
That everyone may eat and drink, and find satisfaction in all
his toil-this is the gift of God.
I know everything that God does will endure forever; nothing
can be added to it and nothing taken from it.
God does it so that men will revere him.
Whatever is has already been, and what will be has been before; and
God will call the past to account.   Ecclesiastes 3:1-15 (NIV)

"Self-Reflection"

What message did you get from Great Words of Wisdom? How can you apply that message to your life?

_____
_____
_____
_____
_____
_____
_____
_____
_____
_____
_____
_____
_____
_____
_____
_____
_____
_____
_____
_____
_____
_____
_____
_____
_____
_____
_____
_____